WITHDRAWN

WINNIPEG
JUL 2004
PUBLIC LIBRARY

Jokes
for ROASTS
& TOASTS

D1051424

Jokes
for Roasts
& Toasts

Compiled and edited by
Jeff Silverman and Lawrence Morgenstern
Illustrated by Dave Cornell

ECW Press

Copyright © Yuk Yuk's Publishing Inc., 2003

Published by ECW Press
2120 Queen Street East, Suite 200, Toronto, Ontario, Canada M4E 1E2

All rights reserved. No part of this publication may be reproduced, stored in a
retrieval system, or transmitted in any form by any process — electronic,
mechanical, photocopying, recording, or otherwise — without the prior written
permission of the copyright owners and ECW Press.

NATIONAL LIBRARY OF CANADA CATALOGUING IN PUBLICATION DATA

Yuk Yuk's joke books

Contents: v. 1. Classic Jokes. — v. 2. Jokes for roasts and toasts.
— v. 3. Jokes men only tell other men.

ISBN 1-55022-606-1 (v. 1.).— ISBN — 1-55022-605-3 (v. 2.).
ISBN 1-55022-607-X (v. 3.).

1. Wit and humor. I. Yuk Yuk's (Toronto, Ont.)

PN6151.Y84 2003   808.87   C2003-902184-X

Cover and Text Design: Tania Craan
Printing: Transcontinental

This book is set in Imago

DISTRIBUTION
CANADA: Jaguar Book Group, 100 Armstrong Avenue, Georgetown, on L7G 5S4

UNITED STATES: Independent Publishers Group, 814 North Franklin Street,
Chicago, Illinois 60610

PRINTED AND BOUND IN CANADA

ECW PRESS
ecwpress.com

Yuk Yuk's "On Tour" offers all types of comedic entertainment for any
occasion. From major concerts to company parties we deliver the laughs.
Call: Funny Business East: 416-967-6431 Ext. 246
or Funny Business West 403-258-2040.

Preface

How many times have you found yourself in a situation where you had to make a toast or a short speech at somebody's birthday, wedding, or some such occasion? Was it a nerve-racking ordeal? Did you stumble and stammer your way through an agonizing and embarrassing attempt to say something passably witty? Didn't you absolutely hate the guy who was able to pick up the gauntlet you'd dropped and dazzle the crowd with a sparkling oration that was funny and polished? "Who the hell does that blow-hard show-off think he is?" you might have asked yourself as you slunk to the bar and tried to forget your humiliation with a few drinks.

Well, take heart. Yuk Yuk's has come to your rescue. This volume is full of pithy remarks, quotable bon mots, and merciless insults. They will provide you with the cerebral arsenal you need to shine at social occasions. You needn't fear again that moment when you are asked to say a few words on behalf of the bride and groom, the birthday boy, or just the occasion. Then you'll be the one they all look at and ask, "Who the hell does that blow-hard show-off think he is?"

This volume of Yuk Yuk's joke books is divided into two parts. The first part contains party roasts the likes of which would make Dean Martin proud. These roasts are in turn divided into several sections. They are arranged in a fashion that makes it easy to select them according to your liking. The second part contains toasts for all occasions. Some are toasts to celebrate having a drink with a friend or just having a drink. Some are short and sweet; some are lengthy and poetic. Memorize them. Use them. Enjoy them.

PART 1

Roasts

Looks

One good thing about your looks. They're a good cure for the hiccups.

You should be in show biz. You have a real face for radio.

I wouldn't say (ROASTEE'S NAME) is ugly, but when he was born the doctor turned him over and said, "Look, twins."

Then the doctor had the hospital incubator windows tinted.

(TO ROASTEE) Of course, your parents still remember the exact moment you were born . . . because your face stopped all the clocks.

He was such an ugly baby his mother tried to put him up for adoption and keep the placenta.

I'm kidding. His parents loved him right from the start. When (ROASTEE'S NAME) was just one day old, his mother said, "What a treasure." And his father said, "Yeah, let's bury it."

He wasn't breast-fed. His mother just wanted to be good friends.

He once looked out a window and got arrested for mooning.

He got a mud pack once and looked great for a few days. But then the mud fell off.

But, hey, being ugly is no crime. (TO ROASTEE) Good thing too; otherwise, you'd get the chair.

One good thing about (ROASTEE'S NAME): he practices birth control—he leaves the light on.

(TO ROASTEE) Of course, you have no idea how ugly you are. Every time you look in a mirror, your reflection ducks.

I'm just kidding. You look great. You have skin like a baby's bottom . . . covered in diaper rash.

I've seen prettier faces on a pirate flag.

His dog has a sign: "Beware of my master."

He makes onions cry.

(ROASTEE'S NAME) is a very influential person. That's right. I can't tell you how many people try to emulate him . . . at Halloween.

(TO ROASTEE) By the way, it's not Halloween now. Take your mask off.

But seriously, I like the way you look. I even hung your picture from my rearview mirror. It keeps car thieves away.

But you have to be comfortable with how you look. After all, mirrors don't lie. And, lucky for you, they can't laugh either.

When his mother dropped him off at school, she was given a ticket for littering.

His dog even has to fantasize about other legs when it humps his.

(TO ROASTEE) Speaking of dogs, if mine looked like you, I'd shave its butt and teach it to walk backward.

I'm not saying (ROASTEE'S NAME) is ugly, but his mother had to put a pork chop around his neck to get the dog to play with him.

He's a real lady killer. They take one look at him and die of fright.

He's the kind of guy who turns the other cheek . . . which is too bad, because it's even uglier.

He's so ugly he has to get his hand drunk to masturbate.

I don't care if people do think you're ugly; I'd still like a picture of you. I want to tape it to my fork to help me lose weight.

He's a real nature lover. Considering the way he looks, you'd think he'd be pissed off at it.

(TO ROASTEE) Every person has the right to be ugly, but you've abused that right.

He's the epitome of dark and handsome. When it's dark, he's handsome.

We've all seen people who look like (ROASTEE'S NAME) before. But usually we had to pay admission.

(TO ROASTEE) You look like a million dollars . . . all green and wrinkled.

(ROASTEE'S NAME) has kept his youthful complexion . . . spotty.

They say your looks go as you get older. (TO ROASTEE) Which gives you something to look forward to.

(TO ROASTEE) But you're pretty as a picture. I guess that explains why every one wants to hang you.

(TO ROASTEE) Just looking at you, I can't help but wonder. . . . Was anyone else hurt in the accident?

He has the face of a Saint . . . Bernard.

(TO ROASTEE) They say beauty is only skin deep. So what do you say we peel you back and get to the good part?

But there are those who appreciate (ROASTEE'S NAME)'s looks. I know of an office downtown where they put his picture up on the wall . . . right next to the clock so employees won't watch it all day.

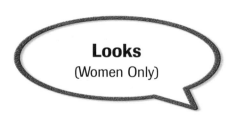

Looks
(Women Only)

She likes to think of herself as a real siren. Actually, she's more of a false alarm.

She's got a face that could make a strap-on dildo go soft.

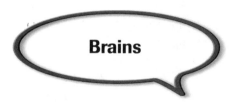

Brains

I'm not saying (ROASTEE'S NAME) is stupid, but he never buys Hamburger Helper because he thinks you need another person to make it.

He's so stupid he can't count his balls and get the same number twice.

I'd call him an idiot, but, hey, we're here to roast him, not pay him compliments.

Many of you think that (ROASTEE'S NAME) is a moron who walks around all the time with nothing on his mind. That's just not true. Sometimes he wears a hat.

He wanted to be a pharmacist when he was a kid, but he didn't know how to get the prescription bottles in the typewriter.

His mother once asked him to go get a color TV, and he asked, "What color?"

He has an answer for everything . . . the wrong one.

He once came up with a great invention . . . a smoke detector with a snooze alarm.

Then he came up with a parachute that opens on impact.

(TO ROASTEE) But you're really special. And I mean that in the Olympic way.

(TO ROASTEE) Have you ever thought of suing your brain for nonsupport?

I'm kidding. (ROASTEE'S NAME) has a mind like a steel trap . . . rusted shut.

He once had a brain transplant, but the brain rejected him.

I've always tried to see things from his point of view. But I just can't stick my head that far up my ass.

No, it's true, he has his head so far up his ass he can chew his food again on the way down.

(ROASTEE'S NAME) has a very calming influence. If you stand close enough to him, you can hear the ocean.

I'm not saying (ROASTEE'S NAME) is brain damaged, but he has to be watered twice a week.

But when I look into his eyes, I can see right through to the back of his head.

But brains aren't everything. (TO ROASTEE) Of course, in your case, they aren't anything.

He doesn't know the meaning of the word fear. But then he doesn't know the meanings of most words.

One good thing about (ROASTEE'S NAME): he's not a hothead. That's for sure. Even his IQ is room temperature.

But he's not a complete idiot. Some parts are missing.

He once took an IQ test . . . and the results were negative.

His gene pool could use a little chlorine.

He's slower than a herd of turtles stampeding through peanut butter.

He's a few fries short of a Happy Meal.

He had a good idea once . . . but it died of loneliness.

But there's a reason (ROASTEE'S NAME) is like this. He was deprived of a lot of things in his childhood. I believe oxygen tops the list.

He's so empty-headed he thinks people are always repeating themselves because of the echo.

His solar panels are aimed at the moon.

He's got a tattoo on his head: "This space for rent."

He's so dense light bends around him.

He tried sniffing coke once, but the ice cubes got stuck in his nose.

If brains were lard, he'd have to boil his bacon (if you know what I mean).

If they taxed intelligence, he'd get a hefty rebate.

If brains were water, he couldn't baptize a flea.

They say what you don't know won't hurt you. That makes (ROASTEE'S NAME) pretty much invulnerable.

You've heard the expression "Penny for your thoughts?" Well, with (ROASTEE'S NAME), you'd get change.

But he's not intellectually challenged . . . provided you don't ask him to spell "intellectually challenged."

You've heard the expression "The lights are on, but nobody's home"? Well, in (ROASTEE'S NAME)'s case, electricity hasn't even been discovered yet.

He's never had a head cold in his life . . .
because germs can't live in a vacuum.

**In bakers' terms, he's a little shy of a dozen.
Not much—just 12.**

He may not look like much, but believe it or not
he shows up many of the great thinkers of our
age. Well, maybe I'm exaggerating. But at least
he's disproved Darwin's theory of evolution.

**He's popular with astronomers. They put a
lens in each ear, and, presto, they have a
telescope.**

He's so dim that his psychic has to use a
flashlight.

**He's so stupid that mind readers charge him
only half price.**

He's got a real Teflon brain. Nothing sticks.

**That twinkle in his eyes . . . is actually the
sun shining between his ears.**

I'm not saying he's dumb, but he thinks $E=MC^2$ is a rap star.

He thinks Moby Dick is a kind of venereal disease.

His train of thought derailed at the station.

He really knows how to use his head . . . to keep the rain off his neck.

When they were handing out brains, he was at the front of the line . . . and ended up holding the door open.

He has a photographic memory. Unfortunately, there's no film in it.

He's been described as open-minded . . . which is better than saying empty-headed.

He's not too handy. He couldn't fix his brakes, so he made his horn louder.

He has a great motto: If at first you don't succeed, maybe skydiving isn't for you.

He has a *Titanic* intellect. It sank the first time out.

If he had half a brain, his ass would be lopsided.

He thinks Meow Mix is a CD for cats.

His brain is like a BB in a moving van.

He thinks a sanitary belt means drinking booze from a clean glass.

He thinks sexual battery is something that comes in a dildo.

He thinks the Internet is something you catch fish in.

He was invited to join a car pool, and he showed up in a bathing suit.

His doctor once told him he wanted to give him a urine test . . . so he studied for three weeks.

He once sent an order of sushi back and complained that it was undercooked.

It takes him two hours to watch *60 Minutes*.

He once got stuck on a broken escalator.

He's so dumb he once climbed over a glass wall to see what was on the other side.

He's the kind of guy who likes to let his mind wander. The only problem is it wandered off and never came back.

He's so stupid he sits on the TV and watches the couch.

His teacher once told the class to make a family tree . . . so he went outside and got some leaves.

He watches *The Three Stooges* and takes notes.

He thought Taco Bell was a Mexican phone company.

He thinks menopause is a button on a DVD player.

He thinks MCI is a rapper.

In closing, I'd like to leave you with one thought . . . but I'm not sure you have anywhere to put it.

But one thing's for sure, (ROASTEE'S NAME) is pretty frugal. When he wanted to save money redecorating his house, he walked around naked for a few days, and his neighbors all chipped in for new curtains.

(ROASTEE'S NAME) may be a tad over-weight, but there are still people who love him anyway . . . Greenpeace.

I had to take a train and two buses just to get on his good side.

He's a light eater. Once it's light, he begins eating.

(ROASTEE'S NAME) was diagnosed with flesh-eating disease. Doctors have given him 20 years to live.

He once jumped up and made the CD player skip . . . at the radio station.

(ROASTEE'S NAME) was crossing the road to visit me one time just as I was driving home, so I had to swerve to avoid hitting him. I ran out of gas.

And his ass is so fat they still haven't found the last chair he was sitting on.

He doesn't put on airs. Hell, the way he eats, he can barely put on pants.

(ROASTEE'S NAME) was so impressed with his chin he added several more.

I'm not saying he's fat, but he once jumped up in midair . . . and got stuck.

He once went on a diet. Three hundred farmers declared bankruptcy.

I'm not saying he's fat, but his driver's license photo was taken with a satellite camera.

If he weighed five more pounds, he could get group insurance.

His blood type is RAGU.

What can I say about (ROASTEE'S NAME)? By and large, he's bi and large.

Baldness

(ROASTEE'S NAME) is self-conscious about his hair. I don't know why—he doesn't have any.

He tries to overcompensate by combing his back hair over.

At least you're saving money on shampoo.

He used to have wavy hair . . . until the day it waved good-bye.

Hairiness

WOMEN

By the way, folks, in case you're wondering, she doesn't have two Greek guys in a headlock. That's her underarm hair.

She shaves her legs with that new feminine product . . . Lady Weed Whacker.

(ROASTEE'S NAME) is a real financial whiz. She once caused the bottom to fall out of the wig market . . . by shaving her legs.

MEN

But (ROASTEE'S NAME) is a great guy. He'd give you the hair off his back.

I wouldn't say (ROASTEE'S NAME) is hairy, but when he was born his mother almost died of rug burns.

He often gets confused with a movie star . . . Chewbacca.

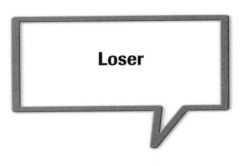

Loser

He's so unlucky, if he ever found the blue bird of happiness, it would mistake him for a statue.

He's not the best at business either. If he bought a cemetery, people would stop dying.

He has one simple motto: If at first you don't succeed, that's par for the course.

He started out with nothing . . . and still has most of it left.

He had to leave his last job due to illness. His boss got sick of him.

He's about as useful as a sunroof in a submarine.

No, seriously, though, whenever something goes wrong at work, he's always got the answer. He sums up the problem with one quick assessment: "It was my fault."

But I'll tell you, success hasn't changed this guy one bit . . . or even come anywhere near him, for that matter.

But (ROASTEE'S NAME) is a hard worker. In fact, he works so much he's missed a lot of his kids' most important moments . . . birthdays, graduations, conceptions.

He was very active in high school sports. I'm not sure what position he played. I think the coach called him one of the team's drawbacks.

He has an inferiority complex . . . and it's fully justified.

I wouldn't say (ROASTEE'S NAME) masturbates a lot, but he had carpel tunnel syndrome reclassified as a sexually transmitted disease.

He's a real animal lover—at least he was until the court order.

But really, (ROASTEE'S NAME), you're a great guy. You should go far. That's not a prediction; it's a request.

He has no equal. Everybody is better.

I'll never forget the first time I met (ROASTEE'S NAME). But I'm hoping the therapy will eventually work.

He can get carried away sometimes. The only problem is it's never far enough.

But he's the kind of guy people enjoy running into . . . when they're driving.

But seriously, (ROASTEE'S NAME) hasn't been himself lately. Have you noticed the improvement?

They gave me five minutes to tell you all the great things about (ROASTEE'S NAME) . . . which is fine, but what will I do for the other four minutes and 50 seconds?

Besides, why should I say nice things about him? I'd rather tell the truth.

Say what you will about (ROASTEE'S NAME); sometimes we all need what only he can provide—his absence.

I love this guy. I remember throwing him a big going-away party . . . but he didn't take the hint.

And, as for all your friends, well, they said you were out of this world. Oh, wait, I'm sorry, I meant "wished."

Some people bring happiness wherever they go. (ROASTEE'S NAME) does the same thing . . . whenever he goes.

(TO ROASTEE) Let's play house. You be the door, and I'll slam you.

He has only one bad habit . . . breathing.

But, (ROASTEE'S NAME), I want you to know, if you ever need a friend, I'd be more than happy to go find you one.

After all, any friend of yours . . . is obviously a poor judge of character.

No, really, I love the guy. I worship the quicksand he walks on.

Some people climb the ladder of success. (ROASTEE'S NAME) walked under it.

He's a guy who always speaks his mind . . .
which explains the long silences.

He once called the suicide hotline. They told him he was doing the right thing.

(ROASTEE'S NAME) is a real self-made man . . .
which means he has no one else to blame.

(TO ROASTEE) In spite of what's been said here tonight about you, just remember we're not mad at you. We're a little miffed at your parents for having had sex, but we're not mad at you.

He obviously doesn't suffer from split personality. I mean, if he did, why would he use this one?

But I gotta tell ya, when they made (ROASTEE'S NAME), they broke the mold. Then, just to play it safe, they found the guy who made the mold and shot him.

Once when he was younger he ran away from home. His parents sent him word that if he didn't come back . . . all would be forgiven.

(ROASTEE'S NAME) is a real friend. He'd go to the ends of the Earth for you. Problem is he won't stay there.

But seriously, let's do something this weekend. What do you say I take you to the zoo? I could use the reward money.

What can you say about a man who is admired, revered, and loved by everyone? For one thing, such a man wouldn't be caught dead at this asshole's roast.

He's worried nobody will remember him when he's gone. I can think of several reasons why he'll be remembered. He wouldn't like any of them, but he'll be remembered.

There's no middle ground with this guy. Either you hate him, or you detest him.

But I want to tell you, people like (ROASTEE'S NAME) don't grow on trees. They usually swing from them.

(LOOKING AT ROASTEE) Now we know why some animals eat their offspring.

(TO ROASTEE) It was rumored that your mother once had an abortion, and now, as we can all see, it's true.

You know they say you should just be yourself. (LOOKING AT ROASTEE) Ordinarily, that's good advice, but in your case. . . .

I'm not saying he was an unwanted child, but when he started school his mother told him, "If a strange man offers you candy to get into his car, go with him."

But (ROASTEE'S NAME) just wants people to accept him as he is. Which is unusual, because most people want to be liked.

But we're glad that (ROASTEE'S NAME) could be here tonight. Thankfully, someone left his cage open.

You know I think (ROASTEE'S NAME) is a great guy and not an asshole at all . . . but then what's my opinion compared with thousands of others?

He's not exactly the most popular guy. The only place he ever gets invited to is outside.

(TO ROASTEE) You know, I thought of you today. Yeah, I was vomiting.

(TO ROASTEE) I'd like to help you out. Which way did you come in?

(ROASTEE'S NAME) has learned from his parents' mistakes. That's why he uses birth control.

But you have to admit he grows on you . . . like a tumor.

He's not as bad as people think. He's much worse.

People would follow him anywhere . . . mostly out of morbid curiosity.

(TO ROASTEE) I like you. People say I have no taste, but I like you.

He has a real speech impediment . . . his foot.

He has a really low opinion of others. He considers them equals.

He used to be arrogant and obnoxious, but now he's just the opposite . . . obnoxious and arrogant.

I don't know what his problem is, but I'm sure it's hard to pronounce and untreatable.

He's very persuasive on major issues. For instance, people take one look at him, and just like that they're in favor of abortion.

(TO ROASTEE) All that you are, you owe to your parents. I know a good lawyer.

(TO ROASTEE) Tell me, did your parents have any children who lived?

I used to think he was a pain in the neck, but now I have a much lower opinion of him.

When he was a child, his mother wanted to hire someone to take care of him. But the mafia wanted too much money.

(ROASTEE'S NAME) believes people should live for the moment. Of course, we all wish he'd live for a moment.

He's been known to do a lot of soul searching. So far, he hasn't found one.

When he was younger, he was a model. He was the poster boy for birth control.

But every time I see (ROASTEE'S NAME), I look forward to the pleasure of his company. I haven't experienced it yet, but I still look forward to it.

Isn't he great? He really lights up a room . . . whenever he leaves it.

He has a very noble purpose in life . . . to serve as a warning to others.

The only reason he's here tonight is because murder is illegal.

He puts the FUN in dysFUNctional.

It's hard to believe that, out of millions of sperm, he was the fastest.

He's living proof that anal sex produces children.

He hasn't been the same since they changed his medication. (TO ROASTEE) By the way, check the bottle. I think it's *two every eight* hours (not the other way around).

Miscellaneous

DAIS INTRO

Before I introduce our guest of honor, I'd like to present some people who want to pay loving tribute to him. We couldn't find any, so we got these losers.

ARROGANT

You know what the difference between (ROASTEE'S NAME) and God is? God doesn't go around acting like he's (ROASTEE'S NAME).

His mind may have gone on vacation, but his mouth is still working overtime.

BAD BREATH

His breath is so bad his dentist will only treat him over the phone.

No, c'mon, that's just a joke. I don't know how his breath smells. I got too close, and my nose was singed shut.

I don't know whether to offer you gum or toilet paper.

Believe me, people aren't saying you're full of shit because they don't agree with your opinions.

BAD LOVER

MEN

He's one of the world's great lovers. All he needs is a partner.

He broke up with his last girlfriend because she wasn't his type . . . inflatable.

He has a pretty pathetic love life. Even hookers tell him they just want to be friends.

The last time he felt a breast it was in a bucket of KFC.

He had a girlfriend once, but they broke up. She chewed through the ropes.

WOMEN

And talk about lousy lays. She fakes orgasms while masturbating.

BAD TEETH
. . . .

But (ROASTEE'S NAME) believes in good hygiene. He goes to the dentist twice a year . . . one time for each tooth.

No, I'm kidding. He has wonderful teeth. And they're all his. He just made the last payment.

BIG NOSE
. . . .

His nose is so big kids are always trying to feed it peanuts.

(TO ROASTEE) I'll bet you open letters with that nose.

BOOBS
. . . .

(TO ROASTEE) I got a joke that'll knock the tits off you. Oh, wait, I see you've heard it already.

(TO ROASTEE) I look at your boobs and remember that zeppelin race that ended in a photo finish.

(TO ROASTEE) Whatever you do, don't get excited. You'll turn your milk into butter.

BORING
. . . .

And he's so boring that sheep count him.

(TO ROASTEE) I'm kidding, you're really a great guy. I just wish I knew you when you were alive.

CHEAP
. . . .

Whenever he donates money to charity, he likes to remain anonymous. That's why he never signs his name on the check.

Talk about cheap. He has rubber pockets so he can steal soup.

Not only are his parties bring your own booze, but you have to bring your own ice too.

He turns the stove off when he flips the bacon.

He once told his kids Santa got killed in a midair collision so he wouldn't have to buy them Christmas presents.

But he's not really cheap. He's just saving for a rainy century.

CRAZY

. . . .

Some say he suffers from insanity, but it's not true. He enjoys it.

He used to have a handle on sanity . . . but it broke.

He's also very paranoid. At least that's what the people following him told me.

He doesn't have the strongest grip on what's going on. You might say his reality check bounced.

But at least he doesn't suffer from stress . . . mainly because he's a carrier.

DRUNK
....

(ROASTEE'S NAME) is the kind of guy who's always got his ear to the ground. But enough about his drinking problem.

But I don't want you thinking he's an alcoholic. He's not. He can go hours without touching a drop.

He believes in a balanced diet: a beer in each hand.

He's such a lush that the last time he gave a urine sample there was an olive in it.

He can't die until the government finds a safe place to bury his liver.

I hear his doctor once found traces of blood in his alcohol.

I'm kidding, he hardly touches the stuff. In fact, it only takes one drink to get him drunk. (TO ROASTEE) Which one was it again, the 15th? The 16th?

He once donated some blood to the Red Cross, and they used it to sterilize the instruments.

HYGIENE
....

He likes to put ice down his pants. It keeps the crabs fresh.

Oh, yeah, he's not the most hygienic guy. He changes his underwear every thousand miles.

He gets more clap than a really good juggler.

LAZY
·······

His nickname down at (ROASTEE'S PLACE OF
EMPLOYMENT) is Blister . . . because he shows
up only after the hard work is done.

**I'm just kidding. His fellow employees say he
does the work of three men: Curly, Larry,
and Moe.**

He's good at everything he does. Unfortunately,
he doesn't do anything.

**He's so lazy that he's the only guy I
know who doesn't walk in his sleep.
He hitchhikes.**

LIAR
·······

You can always tell when (ROASTEE'S NAME)
is lying. His lips move.

OLD

He's so old that his back goes out more than he does.

When he was younger, he sowed his wild oats. Now his wild oats are shredded wheat.

When he was a kid, people asked him what he wanted to be when he was older. (TO ROASTEE) Now, if you answered "Wrinkled," mission accomplished.

His teeth are like stars. They come out at night.

He's so old he has to put his dick in the freezer to get it hard.

PENIS

The man will always be young at heart . . . and at genitals—he's hung like a 10 year old.

His dick is so small it looks like he has two belly buttons.

He was once charged with exposing himself in public, but the case was dismissed due to lack of evidence.

His dick is so small he has to use a pair of tweezers to piss.

He's the only male who has penis envy.

PERVERT
. . . .

His hands are registered with the police . . . the sex offender squad.

I'm just kidding. He does have something registered with the police as a weapon, though. His breath.

RELATIVES

(ROASTEE'S NAME) comes from a tightly knit family. His parents were very close. In fact, they were first cousins.

Which reminds me, I wanted to check his family tree, and it cost $5,000. It was $1,000 to look it up and $4,000 to hush it up.

(TO ROASTEE) Oh, by the way, on your family tree . . . you're the sap.

SLOB

He's not the most refined guy. I was at his house last week. I asked him where the bathroom was, and he said, "Pick a corner."

SHADINESS

A few years ago, he was making really big money . . . about an eighth of an inch too big, which is how the feds caught him.

But (ROASTEE'S NAME) isn't the kind of person to talk about you behind your back. Oh, he'll stab you there, but he'll never talk about you there.

Of course, he always brags about his property in Las Vegas. Yeah, Caesar's Palace is holding his luggage.

But he never met a man he didn't like . . . screwing over.

SHORT

And I'm not saying (ROASTEE'S NAME) is short, but he once almost drowned in a puddle.

(TO ROASTEE) What's it like being the last one to know when it's raining?

Of course, he's sensitive about his height, so don't tease him about it . . . or he'll punch you in the knee.

UPTIGHT
....

(ROASTEE'S NAME) is such a tight ass that when he farts only dogs can hear it.

He could swallow a piece of coal and shit a diamond.

AND FINALLY
....

(AFTER FINAL PERSONAL THOUGHTS) So, before I go, I just want to mention one other thing, buddy. Always remember, when everything is coming your way, you're driving on the wrong side of the road again.

PART 2
Toasts

Wedding Toasts

The wedding toasts are divided into three sections. The first section, "Sentimental and Sincere," contains quaint, old-fashioned toasts that will bring a smile to all assembled. The second section, "Tongue-in-Cheek," includes more humorous, slightly irreverent, toasts that will bring a laugh to most and probably won't be considered inappropriate. The third section, "Risqué," contains, well, risqué toasts that you should do only if you know the wedding guests can handle them or if you are drunk enough to get away with it.

Sentimental and Sincere Wedding Toasts

Here's to the bride that is to be.
Here's to the groom she'll wed.
May all their troubles be light as air
or the feathers that will make up their bed.

May you live as long as you want and never want as long as you live.

May the warmth of your affections survive the frost of old age.

May you always look forward with pleasure and backward with no regrets.

May you grow old on the same pillow.

**Here's to the happy couple that resemble a pair of scissors:
joined so they cannot be separated,
often moving in opposite directions,
but woe to anyone who tries to come between them.**

Let's drink to love . . .
which is nothing until it's multiplied by two.

**To the bride and groom . . .
May today's wedding ceremony be considered no big deal compared to your 50th-anniversary party.**

May the most you wish for be the least you get.

As you travel down life's highway, may all the traffic lights be green.

May the roof above you never fall in and the friends gathered below it never fall out.

**Tongue-in-Cheek
Wedding Toasts**

To the new bride and groom . . .
Never go to bed angry; stay up and fight.

**To marriage . . .
the rest period between romances.**

Marriage is mind over matter.
If he/she doesn't mind, then it doesn't matter.

**To marriage . . .
the mourning after the knot before.**

Here's to marriage . . .
To some it's a small word; to some it's a long
sentence.

To marriage . . .
The only hunt where the trapped animal has to buy the license.

May your children have wealthy parents.

To marriage . . .
The only war where you sleep with the enemy.

To marriage . . .
The process of finding out what kind of
person your spouse would really have
preferred.

Marriage is when a man and a woman become as one.
The trouble begins when they try to decide which one.

Marriage means commitment . . .
but then so does insanity.

To marriage . . .
The institute that confers a very special privilege: only married people can get divorced.

To marriage . . .
life's three-ring circus: engagement ring,
wedding ring, suffer ring.

To marriage . . .
For the bride, it means a shower; for the
groom, it means curtains.

All marriages are happy.
It's the living together afterward that causes all
the problems.

A husband expects his wife to be perfect . . .
and understand why he's not.

Here's to the groom . . .
living proof that (BRIDE'S NAME) can take
a joke.

A husband should never question his wife's
judgment.
After all, look whom she married.

A wedding ring is like a tourniquet.
It cuts off circulation.

Confucius says, "A man who sinks in a woman's arms soon has arms in a woman's sink."

To the groom . . .
Here's to your new bride, who has
everything a girl could want in life except good
taste in men.

To the bride and groom . . .
Here's a little tip for the groom: if she ever wants to learn how to drive, don't stand in her way.

Here's to (GROOM'S NAME) . . .
To you being in total control—just don't tell
(BRIDE'S NAME).

May you be too good for the world and not good enough for your wife.

May you grow so rich that your wife's
second husband never has to worry about making a living.

(TO BRIDE) Put your hand on the table.
(TO GROOM) Now put your hand on top of
(BRIDE'S NAME'S) hand.
Now everyone raise your glass, and let's all
drink a toast to the last time (GROOM'S
NAME) has the upper hand.

Marriage is a great university. It teaches you
patience, consideration, understanding, and all
sorts of other crap you wouldn't need if you
remained single.

A wedding is like a funeral except you get to
sniff your own flowers.

To keep a marriage brimming
with love in the loving cup,
when you are wrong admit it,
and when you are right shut up.

Always remember, in any argument or
disagreement, the husband is entitled to
the last few words.
And those words are "Yes, dear."

To the two secrets of a long-lasting, happy marriage . . .
a sense of humor and a short memory.

To the bride . . .
May she share everything with her husband, including the housework.

Here's to King Solomon, ruler and sage,
the wisest of men in history's page.
He had wives by the hundreds and thought it was fun—
here's hoping you'll know how to handle just one.

Congratulations on the termination
of your isolation,
and may I express an appreciation
of your determination
to end the desperation
and frustration
that have caused you so much consternation
in giving you the inspiration
to make a combination
to bring an accumulation
to the population.

Here's to happiness . . .
I never knew happiness until I got married . . . and
now it's too late.

To the groom . . .
Here's to the best years of your life,
the years you spent with another man's
wife . . .
your mother.

Here's to matrimony . . .
The high sea for which no compass has been
invented.

Here's to the bride and groom . . .
A case of love pure and simple: the bride is
pure, and the groom is simple.

Here's to marriage . . .
for a man isn't complete until he's married . . .
and then he's finished.

To your marriage . . .
May your love grow as surely as your waist-
line will.

Marriage is a wonderful institution.
But who wants to live in an institution?

**Here's to the bride's mother, who calls the
groom "son" . . .
but only because he never let her finish her
sentence.**

Here's to a love,
a love that will linger.
He gave her the ring . . .
and she gave him the finger.

**Love is blind.
Marriage is the eye-opener.**

Here's to the sign in the marriage
counselor's window . . .
"Out to lunch. Think it over."

**Some women marry men thinking they're
real comforters . . .
only to discover that they're merely wet
blankets.**

Here's to the bride . . .
May you be blessed with many children.
And here's to your new husband . . .
The only one of your children who won't grow up and move away.

Here's to women . . .
They get all excited about nothing . . .
and then they marry him.

Here's to marriage being a wonderful partnership . . .
And to the husband . . . the silent partner.

Here's to the groom, with a bride so sweet and fair . . .
a lovely young lass to whom none can compare.
And here's to the bride. . . .

Here's to marriage, although I wonder why we bother.
Just find a woman you hate and buy her a house.

Here's to a husband who stands by his wife when she's in trouble she wouldn't be in if she wasn't married to him.

Here's to a joint checking account . . .
a handy little device that permits a wife to beat her husband to the draw.

Here's to love . . .
an obsessive compulsion cured by marriage.

Here's to a wedding ring . . .
the world's smallest handcuff.

Here's to (BRIDE'S NAME) . . .
Before she found her handsome prince, she had to kiss a lot of frogs.

Here's to a wife . . .
the perfect acquisition for the man who believes he has too much control of his own affairs.

Here's to marriage . . .
Without it, men and women would have to
fight with total strangers.

Here's to your husband being like a fine wine
and improving with age.
Just lock him in the basement.

Here's to marriage being like a violin.
It sounds good, but there are strings
attached.

Here's to having a mother-in-law . . .
who will destroy your mind by giving you a piece
of hers.

Here's to the bride and groom . . .
They've come up with a perfect compromise.
He won't try to run her life . . . and he won't
try to run his either.

Here's to the best way to keep a man . . .
behind bars.

Risqué Wedding Toasts

Your new bride will now expect a mink.
(TO BRIDE) You know how to get minks, don't
you? The same way that minks get minks.

**May all your ups and downs be between the
sheets.**

The vows have been made,
the cake has been cut.
Let's hope that the bride
doesn't grow a big butt.

Here's to the bride . . .
She'll soon lose her cherry, but that's no sin,
for she's saving the box that it came in.

Congratulations on finding a socket for your
plug. (OR plug for your socket.)

Here's to the wedding night . . .
If done right, it's like a chicken dinner: a
 little leg, a little breast, and a lot of stuffing.

To the new couple . . .
Just a bit of advice: you can't treat each other
like doormats . . . .
unless you both lie down.

Always talk to your wife during
lovemaking . . .
if there's a phone handy.

A gentleman is someone who never swears at
his wife when there are ladies present.

A good woman is like a good bar . . .
liquor in the front and poker in the rear.

To the honeymoon . . .
If it goes right, it's just like a bridge table: four
bare legs and no drawers.

To the new bride . . .
Whatever you do, don't keep your husband
in the doghouse too long. He might give his
bone to the woman next door.

Easy on the throttle,
steady on the gears.
Roll her over gently,
and she'll last for many years.

(BRIDE'S NAME), we had (GROOM'S NAME) at our company for years. He was useless in every position. Hopefully, you'll have better luck.

Life's a bitch . . .
and then you marry one.

Here's to getting married . . .
It's like buying a dishwasher: you never have to do it by hand again.

Life sucks . . .
and then you marry someone who doesn't.

Here's to the newlyweds' journey being a thousand miles long . . .
and coming in six-inch installments.

Here's to the bride and groom . . .
He offered his honor,
she honored his offer,
and all night long,
he was on 'er and off 'er.

Sugar in the bowl,
coffee in the cup.
Poke her in the butt,
and you won't knock her up.

Never make love by the garden gate.
Love may be blind, but the neighbors ain't.

To our wives and lovers . . .
May they never meet.

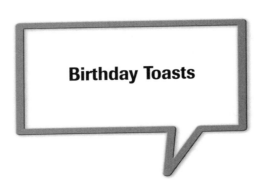

Birthday Toasts

May you be poor in misfortune,
rich in blessings,
slow to make enemies,
and quick to make friends.

**May bad fortune follow you all the days of
your life . . .
and never catch up to you.**

May the people who dance on your grave get
cramps in their legs.

May your house always be too small to hold all your friends.

May your wealth be like the capital of Ireland . . . always Dublin.

You're not too old when your hair turns gray. You're not too old when your teeth decay. You'll know that it's time for that final sleep, when your mind makes promises your body can't keep.

You're not as young as you used to be. But you're not as old as you're going to be.

To a great age . . . old enough to know better, young enough not to care.

The trick to getting older is to live each moment as if it were your last . . . because sooner or later it will be.

Here's to birthdays . . .
They're not so bad considering the
alternative.

A man is only as old as the woman he feels.

May your life be like toilet paper . . .
long and useful.

Happy birthday.
May you live to be a hundred years . . . with one
extra year to repent.

Happy birthday.
As you slide down the banister of life, may
the splinters never point the wrong way.

May the best day of your past be the worst day
of your future.

Another candle in your cake;
well, that's no cause to pout.
Be glad that you still have the strength,
to blow the damn things out.

Here's hoping that you live forever and that mine
is the last voice you hear.

**May you die in bed at 100 . . .
shot by a jealous husband.**

Here's to you . . .
No matter how old you are, you don't look it.

**Here's to you, old friend, may you live a
thousand years,
just to sort of cheer things up, in this vale of
human tears.
And may I live a thousand too—a thousand
less a day,
because I wouldn't want to be on Earth and
hear you'd passed away.**

To your birthday,
glass held high.
Glad it's you who's older,
and not I.

Another year older?
Just think this way.
You're only one day older
than yesterday.

A toast to your coffin . . .
May it be made of 100-year-old oak, and may we
plant the tree together tomorrow.

Friendship Toasts

**Here's to champagne to our real friends
and real pain to our sham friends.**

To a beautiful wife, a good job . . .
and friends to keep you from blowing it all.

**Friends we are today,
and friends we'll always be.
For I am wise to you,
and you can see through me.**

May the dust from your tires blind the eyes of
your enemies.

May your troubles be as few and far between as my grandmother's teeth.

Here's to our friends . . .
and the strength to put up with them.

Here's to absent friends, and here's twice to absent enemies.

The Lord gives us relatives.
Thank God we can choose our friends.

**To our friends . . .
who know the truth about us but refuse to believe it.**

Here's to never breaking plans to go out with a guy/girl.

**Here's to you, and here's to me,
in the hope we never disagree.
But if we do, the hell with you—
here's to me.**

I've drunk to your health in taverns,
I've drunk to your health at home,
I've drunk to your health so many damn times,
I believe I've ruined my own.

May your liquor be cold.
May your women be hot.
May your troubles slide off you
slicker than snot.

May you . . .
work like you don't need the money,
love like you've never been hurt,
dance like no one is watching,
screw like it's being filmed,
and drink like an Irishman.

Here's health to your enemies' enemies.

May you fall on something with few corners.

May misfortune cookies follow you the rest
of your life . . .
and may you never learn to read them.

Here's to those who wish us well . . .
As for the rest, they can go to hell.

**Here's to a long life and a merry one,
a quick death and an easy one,
a pretty girl and an honest one,
a cold drink and another one.**

May you never forget what is worth
remembering
or remember what is best forgotten.

**Here's to health and prosperity,
to you and all your posterity,
and to those who don't drink with sincerity,
may they be damned for all eternity.**

Here's to more friends and to less of them.

Drinking Toasts

Here's to women's kisses,
and to whisky amber and clear,
not as sweet as a woman's kiss,
but a damn sight more sincere.

I'd rather have a bottle in front of me than a frontal lobotomy.

Thirst is a shameless disease, so here's to a shameful cure.

Give a man a fish, and he'll eat for a day. Teach a man to fish, and he'll sit in a boat all day and drink beer.

Draft beer, not people.

**Here's to reality . . .
an illusion that occurs due to lack of
alcohol.**

Here's to the woman who drove me to drink.
I never even thanked her.

**Drink what you want, drink what you're able.
If you're drinking with me, you'll be under
the table.**

Here's to booze . . .
It makes other people interesting.

**Here's to beer . . .
It goes through you so quickly because it
doesn't have to stop and change color.**

Some Guinness was spilled on the barroom floor,
as the pub was closed for the night.
Out from his hole crept a wee brown mouse,
and stood in the pale moonlight.
He lapped up the frothy brew from the floor,
and back on his haunches he sat.
And all night long you could hear him roar,
"Bring on the goddamn cat!"

Here's to beer . . .
much better than religion. You don't have
to wait 2,000 years for a second beer.

Pity the people who don't drink.
When they wake up in the morning, that's the
best they're going to feel all day.

Life is a waste of time,
and time is a waste of life.
So get wasted all of the time,
and have the time of your life.

Eat, drink, and be merry . . .
for tomorrow we may not be able to afford it.

To consciousness . . .
that annoying time between blackouts.

Best while you have it to use your breath . . .
for there is no drinking after death.

Here's to abstinence . . .
as long as it's practiced in moderation.

A light heart lives long, but your liver will give out long before then.

May the floor rise up to meet you.

Of all my favorite things to do,
the utmost is to have a brew.
My love grows for my foamy friend,
with each thirst-quenching elbow bend.
Beer's so frothy, smooth, and cold . . .
it's paradise—pure liquid gold.
Yes, beer means many things to me . . .
that's all for now. I have to pee.

Being drunk is feeling sophisticated when you can't say it.

To beer . . .
the drink that makes you feel the way you ought to feel without beer.

I have taken more out of alcohol than alcohol has taken out of me.

Everybody should believe in something.
I believe I'll have another drink.

Eat, drink, and be merry . . .
for tomorrow they may cancel your VISA.

I don't have a drinking problem.
I drink, I get drunk, I fall down—no problem.

He who laughs last . . .
hasn't passed out yet.

Sobriety is a condition that can be cured with
alcohol.

To some it's a six-pack.
To me it's a support group.

There are several good reasons for drinking,
and one has just entered my head.
If a man can't drink when he's living,
how the hell can he drink when he's dead?

In heaven there is no beer.
That's why we drink ours here.

Here's head first, in a foaming glass.
Here's head first, to a lovely lass.
Here's head first, for a bit of kissing,
for the good don't know the fun they're missing.

A candidate is an easy man;
he tells his lies by rote.
An elected man invents his lies,
and rams them down your throat.
So stay at home and drink your beer,
and let the neighbors vote.

Times are hard,
and wages are small.
So drink more beer,
and screw them all.

Here's to the good time we'll assume we
had tomorrow.

There are three good reasons why we drink:
good friends, good wine, and any other reason
why.

For every wound, a balm.
For every sorrow, a cheer.
For every storm, a calm.
For every thirst, a beer.

Champagne costs too much,
whisky's too rough,
vodka puts big mouths in gear.
This little refrain,
should help to explain,
why it's better to order a beer.

**God invented whisky so the Irish wouldn't
take over the world.**

When life's too hard,
and seems a bore,
and your spirits seem to be sinking,
just point to the man
who's on the floor
and say, "Give me what he's been drinking."

**The only difference between an Irish
wedding and an Irish wake is one less
drunk.**

When we drink, we get drunk.
When we get drunk, we fall asleep.
When we fall asleep, we commit no sin.
When we commit no sin, we get to heaven.
So let's get drunk . . .
and go to heaven.

Work is the curse of the drinking class.

Thirsty days hath September, April, June, and November.
All the rest are thirsty too,
except for him who hath home brew.

Here's to holding on to the lawn to keep from falling off the Earth.

Here's to drinking and the job it interferes with.

Here's to drinking and your career not progressing beyond senator of Massachusetts.

Here's to the back of your head getting hit by the toilet seat.

Here's to the sincere belief that alcohol is the elusive fifth food group.

Here's to 24 hours in a day and 24 beers in a case.
Coincidence? I don't think so.

Here's to two hands and just one mouth . . . Now that's a drinking problem.

Here's to when you can focus better with one eye closed.

Here's to when every woman you see has an exact twin.

Here's to when you keep asking your wife, "Where are the kids?"
and you're not married, and you're talking to a fridge.

Here's to the next morning, when you discover the cleaning supplies are missing.

Here's to beer . . .
It's not just for breakfast anymore.

Here's to when the glass keeps missing your mouth.

Here's to when you donate blood, and they ask, "What proof?"

Here's hoping vampires get woozy after biting you.

Here's to waking up with a traffic cone between your legs.

Here's to waking up just in time to hear "Do you take this woman?"

Gentlemen . . .
start your livers.

**I used to know a clever toast,
but now I cannot think of it.
But fill your glasses with anything,
and you sons of bitches will drink it.**

To alcohol . . .
the cause of, and solution to, all our problems.

One bottle for the four of us.
Thank God there isn't more of us.

On the chest of a barmaid in Sale
were tattooed the prices of ale.
And on her behind,
for the sake of the blind,
was the same information in braille.

Wine improves with age.
The older I get, the more I like it.

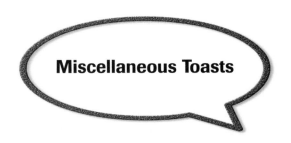

Miscellaneous Toasts

Here's to the best things in life being free and not worth it.

Here's to sex appeal being 50% of what you've got and 50% of what people think you've got.

Here's to sobriety . . .
May it continue to reduce the number of men who think they can sing.

Here's to the man who is wisest and blessed.
Here's to the man whose judgment is best.
Here's to the man as smart as can be—
the man, of course, who agrees with me.

118

Never argue with idiots.
They drag you down to their level and then beat you with experience.

Get on your knees and thank the Lord you're on your feet.

May the Lord love us and call us, but not too soon.

**Here's to the fools of the world . . .
Without them, the rest of us couldn't succeed.**

As you ramble through life,
whatever your goal,
keep your eyes on the doughnut,
and not the hole.

**Here's to poverty . . .
It sticks by when our friends forsake us.**

Like Kermit the Frog once said, "Time is fun when you're having flies."

**May you soar like an eagle . . .
and get sucked into a jet engine.**

When my days are over,
and from this world I pass,
I hope they bury me upside down,
so the world can kiss my ass.

**A toast to our ancestors, who brought us
this far.
May their efforts not be wasted,
and may we do as well by our descendants.**

May God turn our enemies' hearts.
Or, failing that, turn their ankles . . . so we'll
know them by their limping.

**To man . . .
the only animal that laughs,
drinks even when not thirsty,
and mates no matter what the season.**

May you be blessed with a wife so healthy and
strong she can pull the plow when your horse
drops dead.

Hey, hey, at least we're not French.

May your life, your love, your wine, and your jokes be cheap.

Dance as if no one were watching,
sing as if no one were listening,
and live today as if it were your last . . .
because I'll kill you if you don't stop singing
and dancing.

Reality is merely an illusion . . .
albeit a very persistent one.

Here's to housework . . .
What the wife does that nobody notices
until she doesn't do it.

Money can't buy love . . .
but it sure puts you in a great bargaining position.

Here's to diplomacy . . .
the ability to tell a man to go to hell so that
he looks forward to the trip.

A toast to bread . . .
for without bread, there'd be no toast.

**Here's to never marrying a tennis player . . .
for love means nothing to them.**

May you have the hindsight to know where
you've been,
the foresight to know where you're going,
and the insight to know when you've gone too
far.

**The hand that rocks the cradle
is the hand that rules the Earth.
But the hand that holds four aces,
bet on it for all your worth.**

Toasts to the Sexes

There are two theories about arguing with
a woman.
Neither one works.

**Women have many faults,
men have only two:
everything they say,
and everything they do.**

Here's to men of all classes . . .
who, through lasses and glasses,
will make themselves asses.

**Here's to the model wife . . .
usually someone else's.**

Here's to the ladies . . .
They need no praise—they speak for themselves.

Here's to the men . . .
May they end up what they think themselves
to be.

May we kiss whom we please,
and please whom we kiss.

Here's to Cupid, the little squirt.
He lost his pants, he lost his shirt.
He's lost most everything but his aim,
which shows that love is a losing game.

Here's to the women who love me terribly . . .
May they soon improve.

Here's to the man who takes a wife . . .
Let him make no mistake,
for it makes a lot of difference,
depending on whose wife you take.

Here's to all the women who have used and abused me . . .
May they continue to do so.

**Love thy neighbor,
but make sure his wife / her husband is
away first.**

Here's to the wife who thinks her husband is the world's best lover . . .
May she never catch him at it.

**Here's to your opinions being the same as
your wife's.**

Here's to my wife . . .
who doesn't care what I do when I'm away from home—as long as I don't enjoy myself.

**Here's to my wife . . .
who has a split personality—I hate both of
them.**

Here's to my wife . . .
who says she'll leave me if I go fishing one more time. I'm going to miss her.

Here's to my wife . . .
who submits and obeys. She always lets me have her way.

Here's to being a bachelor . . .
and avoiding the opportunity to make some woman miserable.

Here's to bachelors . . .
the only men who never told lies to their wives.

Here's to the man who never tells his wife he's sterile until she's pregnant.

To women . . .
God's greatest gift to and cruelest trick on man.

Here's to love . . .
the only fire there's no insurance for.

A woman never forgets the men she could have had.
A man never forgets the women he couldn't.

Here's to the husband who buys his football tickets four months in advance and waits until December 24th to buy Christmas presents.

Lewd and Crude Toasts

I'll drink to the girls that do,
I'll drink to the girls that don't.
But I won't drink to the girls that say they will,
and then I find out they don't.

**Here's to the guy who goes to work every
day from a different direction.**

Here's to the wings of love . . .
May they never molt a feather
till your little shoes and my big boots
are under the bed together.

Here's to the maiden of 20,
who knows that it's folly to yearn.
So she picks a lover of 50,
because he has money to burn.

Men are much like sausages,
very smooth upon the skin.
But you can never tell how much
hog there is within.

Here's to the girl I love the best . . .
I've loved her naked, and I've loved her
dressed.
I've loved her standing, and I've loved her
lying.
If she had wings, I'd love her flying.
And when she's dead and long forgotten,
I'll dig her up and love her rotten.

Here's to the woman who gave me this.
It hurts each time I take a piss.
If she's around when I get well,
I'll get it again, sure as hell.

**Here's to the breeze that blows through the
trees,
that blows the skirt off a young girl's knees,
which leads to sights that sometimes
please,
but more often leads to social disease.**

I love them, all the ladies,
with their frilly little things.
I love them with their diamonds,
their perfumes, and their rings.
I love them, all the ladies,
I love them big and small.
But when a lady isn't quite a lady,
that's when I love them most of all.

**Here's to panties . . .
not the best thing in the world, but damn
close to it.**

Here's to sleeping triple,
seeing double,
living single,
and testing negative.

Here's to wind . . .
not the kind that brings down shacks and shanties,
the kind that blows off bras and panties.

Here's to Eve, the mother of our race,
wore a fig leaf in just the right place.
Here's to Adam, the father of us all,
knew where to be when the leaves began to fall.

Here's to sex having no calories.

Here's to the perfect girl,
I couldn't ask for more,
A deaf nymphomaniac who owns a liquor store.

To virgins and lesbians . . .
Thanks for NOTHING.

My darling wife was always glum.
I drowned her in a cask of rum.
And so made sure that she would stay
in better spirits night and day.

Here's to the cure for virginity.

Here's to the ships of our navy,
and to the ladies of our land.
May the former be well rigged,
and the latter be well manned.

Here's to the woman of my dreams . . .
who looks like a million—and is just as hard
to make.

Here's to the game they call 10 Toes,
it's played all over town;
the girls all play with 10 toes up,
the boys with 10 toes down.

To your real dad, whoever he may be.

To women and horses . . .
and the men who ride them.

Here's to hell!
May we have as good a time in there as we
spent in getting there.

Always remember . . .
brandy makes you randy,
whisky makes you frisky,
but a good stiff Johnny Walker can make you
pregnant.

Here's to widowhood . . .
the only compensation some women get out
of marriage.

Here's to sex . . .
There are some things better and some things
worse, but there's nothing like it.

Here's to men . . .
If you get them by the balls, their hearts and
minds will follow.

Here's to the Garden of Eden . . .
It wasn't what you were led to believe.
The trouble was not from the apple on the tree
But from the "pair" Adam saw on Eve.

Here's to nice guys finishing last.

Here's to sex . . .
It's only dirty if it's done right.

Here's to sex . . .
one of the nine reasons for reincarnation—
the other eight are unimportant.

Here's to sowing your wild oats on Saturday and
praying for crop failure on Sunday.

Here's to the game of love never being
called on account of darkness.

Here's to swimmin' with bow-legged women.

Here's to darkness . . .
where all women are beautiful.